Head Start

KINDERGARTEN

Contents

Editorial:
Laura Bourbonnais
Emmie Nicholson
Kaelan Ryan
Clarissa Sorgiovanni

Art Direction:
Doran Woo

Design:
Eleonora Fert
Viviane Machado
Doran Woo

Original Illustrations:
Steven Wood

Tracing

Trace the dotted lines from left to right.

Trace the dotted lines from right to left.

LEFT **RIGHT**

If tracing the lines with a pen or pencil is too difficult for your child, they can trace the lines with their index finger first.

Trace and continue the dotted lines from left to right without touching the black lines.

LEFT **RIGHT**

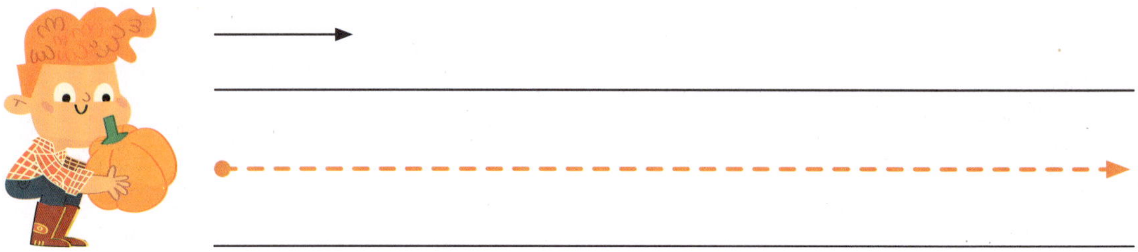

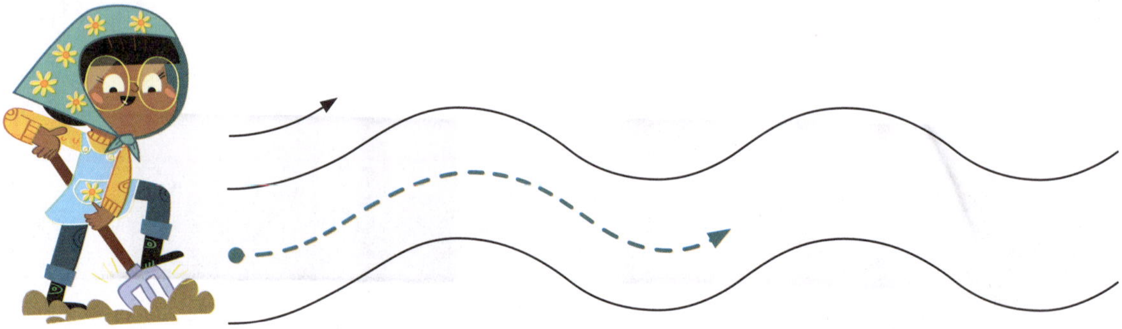

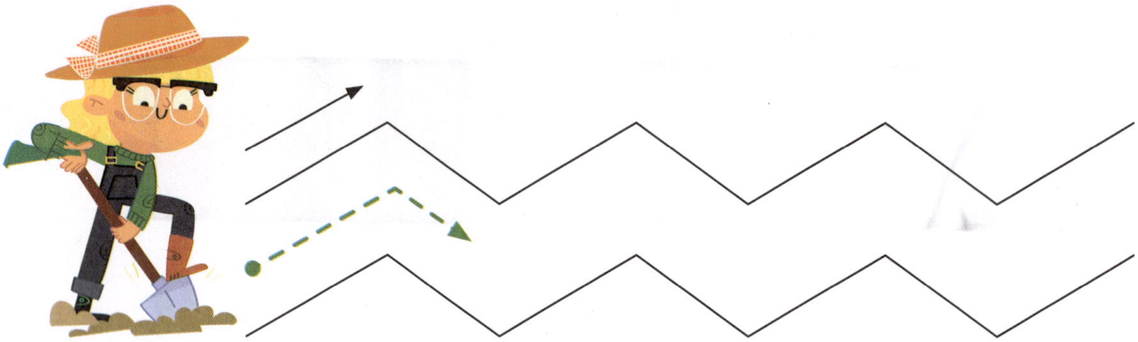

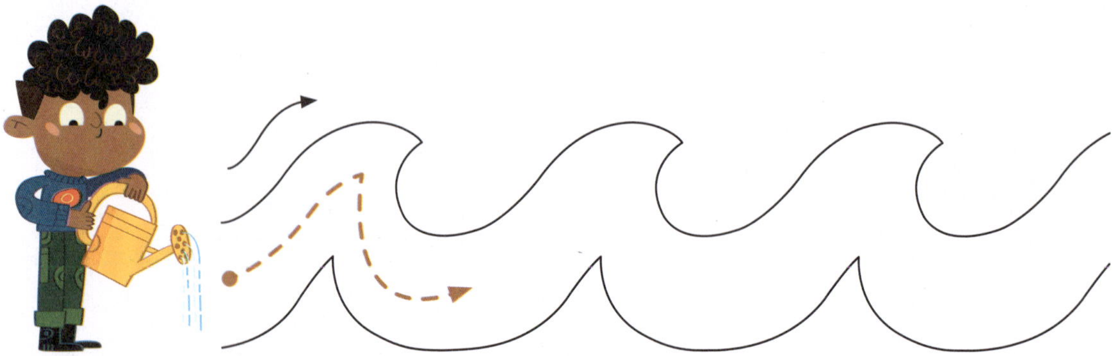

The Letter A

Point to each picture at the bottom of the page and read the word out loud, emphasizing the first letter. Have your child repeat after you.

Trace and print the **uppercase A** and **lowercase a**.

A A A A

a a a a

alien

apple

avocado

Draw a line from right to left without touching the black lines.

LEFT **RIGHT**

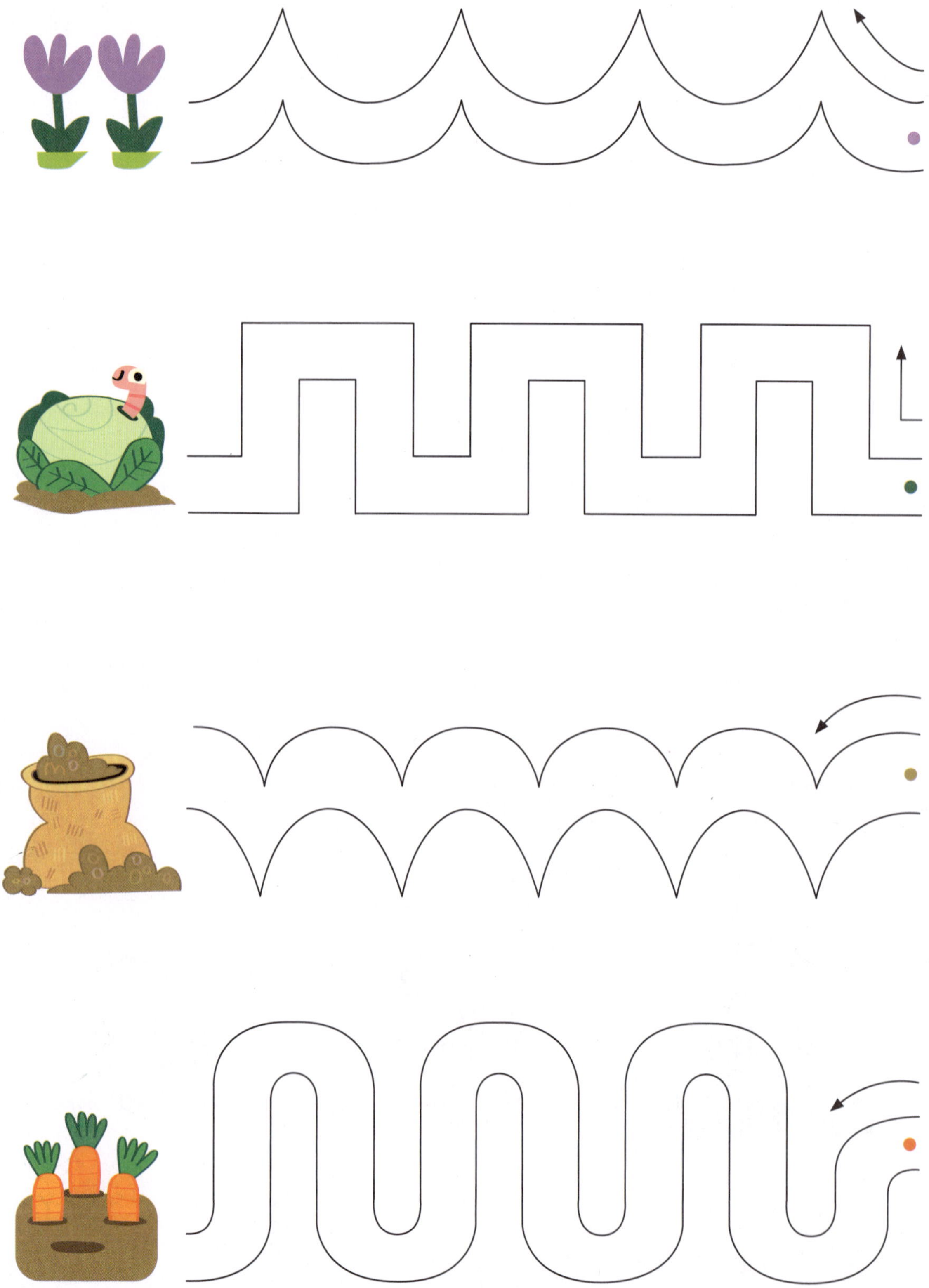

Trace and print the **uppercase B** and **lowercase b**.

B B B B

b b b b

bird

ball

boot

Trace and print the **uppercase C** and **lowercase c**.

C C C C

c c c c

cup

cabbage

comic

Trace and print the **uppercase D** and **lowercase d**.

D D D D

d d d d

dog

dishes

duck

Trace and print the **uppercase E** and **lowercase e.**

eagle

egg

elephant

Trace and print the **uppercase F** and **lowercase f**.

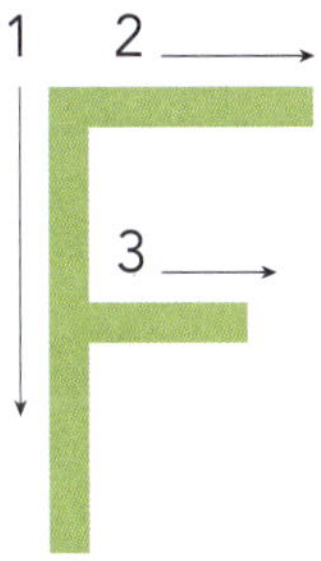

F F F

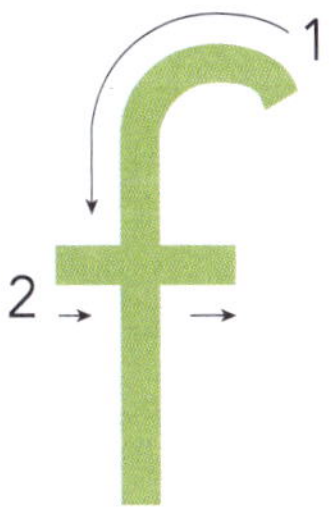

f f f

fire

flowers

fishbowl

Trace and print the **uppercase G** and **lowercase g**.

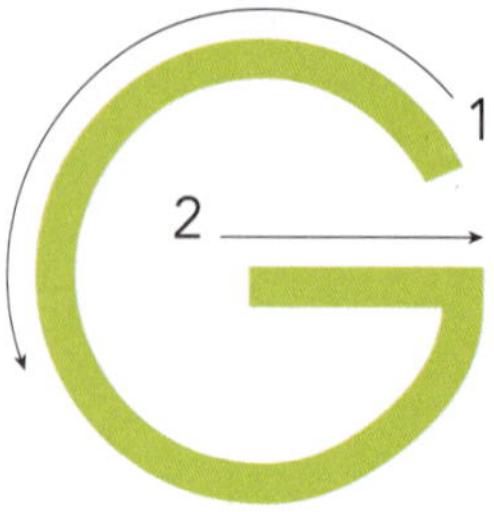

G G G

g g g

globe

girl

glove

Trace and print the **uppercase H** and **lowercase h**.

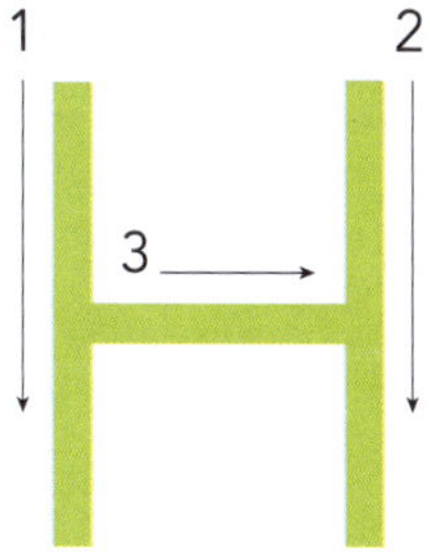

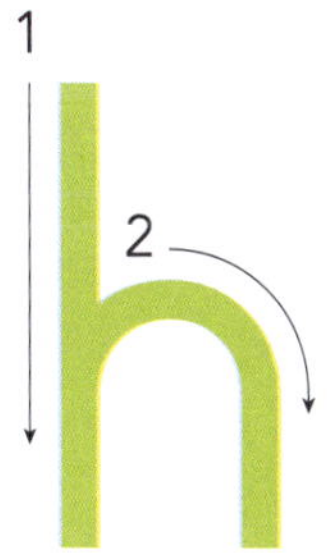

hero

hot dog

house

The Letter H

Ask your child what the first letter of their name is.

Trace and print the **uppercase I** and **lowercase i**.

insect

ice

iguana

Trace and print the **uppercase J** and **lowercase j**.

1

J J J J

2
1

j j j j

juice

jug

jeans

The Letter K

Trace and print the **uppercase K** and **lowercase k**.

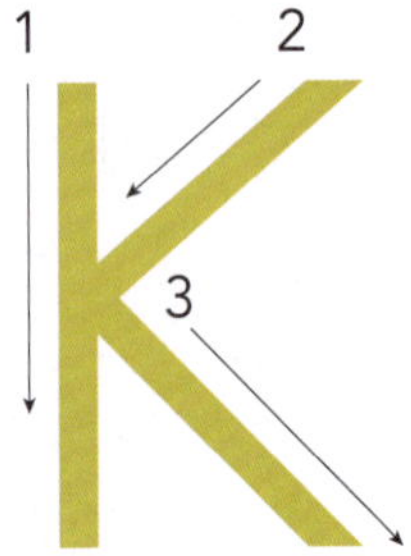

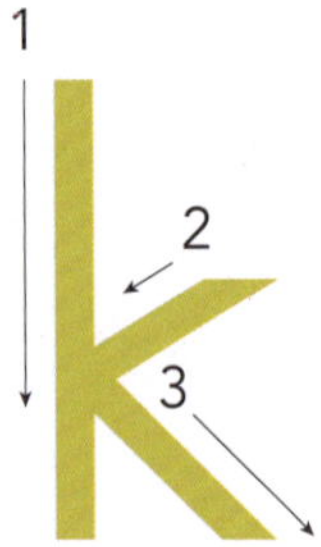

kiwi

koala

kettle

The Letter L

Trace and print the **uppercase L** and **lowercase l**.

1

L

2

1

l

lobster

lamp

leaves

Can your child think of anything else that begins with the letter **L**?

The Letter M

Trace and print the **uppercase M** and **lowercase m**.

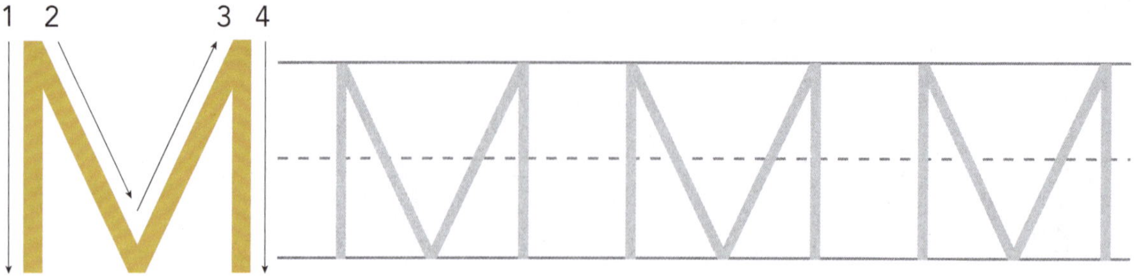

monkey

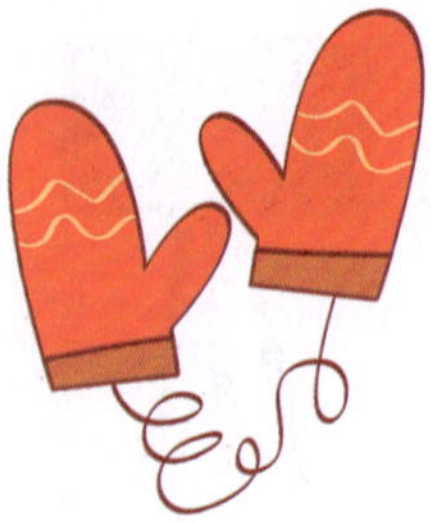

mittens

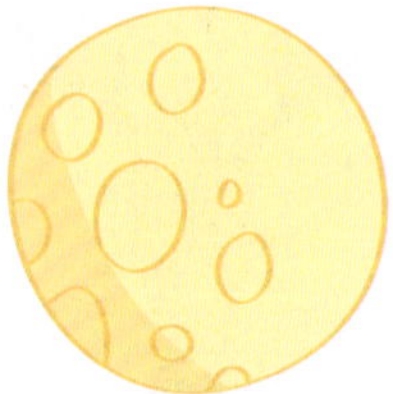

Moon

Trace and print the **uppercase N** and **lowercase n**.

1 2 3

N N N N

1 2

n n n n

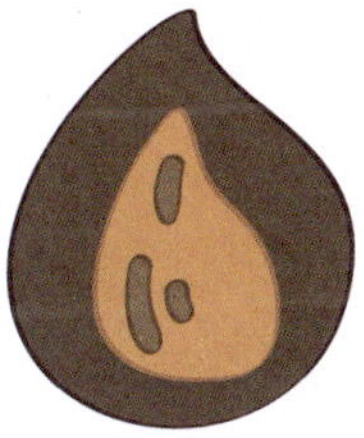

nut

nest

narwhal

Trace and print the **uppercase O** and **lowercase o**.

owl

olive

octopus

Trace and print the **uppercase P** and **lowercase p**.

1 2

P P P P

1 2

p p p p

pot

pizza

planet

The Letter
Q

Trace and print the **uppercase Q** and **lowercase q**.

queen

quail

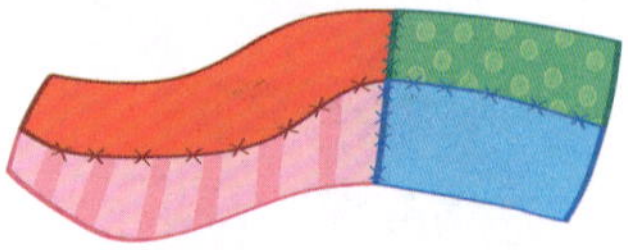

quilt

The Letter
R

Trace and print the **uppercase R** and **lowercase r**.

1 2 3

R R R R

1 2

r r r r

raccoon

radish

rocket

The Letter S

Ask your child to point to something they see that starts with the letter **S**.

Trace and print the **uppercase S** and **lowercase s**.

S S S S

s s s s

scissors

star

sock

Trace and print the **uppercase T** and **lowercase t**.

T-shirt

tree

train

The Letter U

Trace and print the **uppercase U** and **lowercase u**.

1 U U U U

1 2 u u u u

unicorn

umbrella

ukulele

Trace and print the **uppercase V** and **lowercase v**.

1 V 2

V V V

1 v 2

v v v

vest

vehicle

vase

The Letter
W

Trace and print the **uppercase W** and **lowercase w**.

1 2 3 4

W W W

1 2 3 4

w w w w

window

wrench

wheel

Trace and print the **uppercase X** and **lowercase x**.

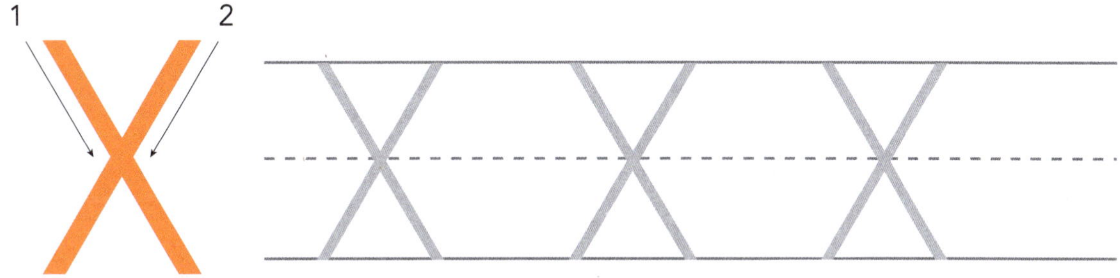

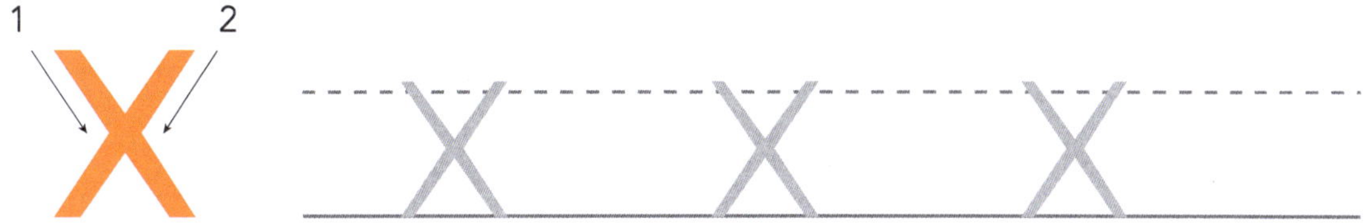

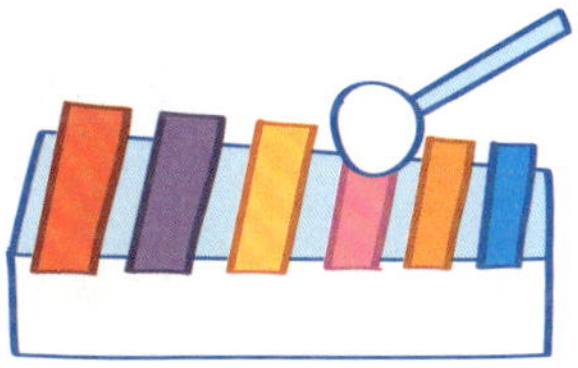
xylophone

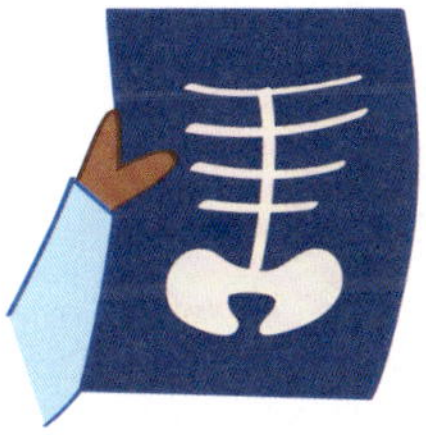
X-ray

The Letter
Y

Trace and print the **uppercase Y** and **lowercase y**.

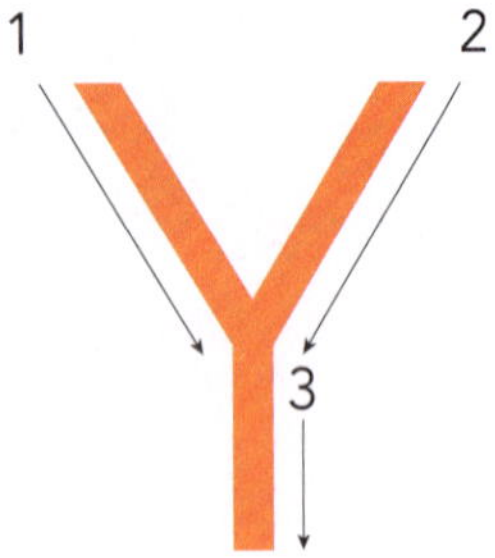

Y Y Y

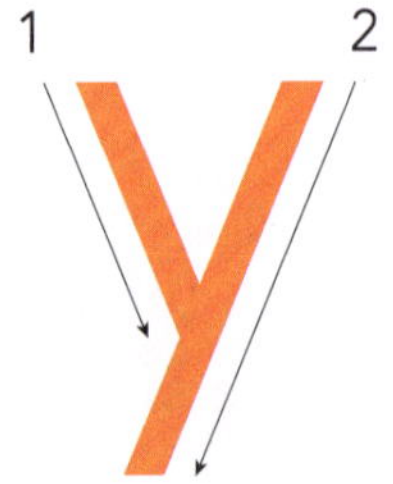

y y y

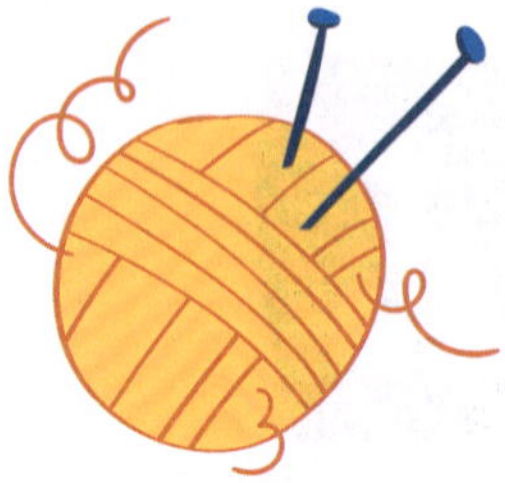

yarn

yogurt

yak

Trace and print the **uppercase Z** and **lowercase z**.

Z Z Z Z

z z z z

zucchini

zipper

zebra

The Letter Z

Z is the least commonly used letter in English!

Trace the letters from A to Z.

Aa Bb

Cc Dd

Ee Ff

Gg Hh

Ii Jj

Kk Ll

Mm Nn

Trace the letters from A to Z.

Oo Pp

Qq Rr

Ss Tt

Uu Vv

Ww Xx

Yy Zz

ABCDEFGHIJKLMNOPQRSTUVWXYZ

abcdefghijklmnopqrstuvwxyz

Letters
A–Z

Bookmark this page and refer to it when your child needs help remembering the order of the alphabet.

Connect the Dots

After your child has connected the dots, they can colour the drawing with crayons or markers!

Connect the dots from A to Z to complete the picture.

Connect the dots from A to Z to complete the picture.

If your child gets stuck, refer to the alphabet on page 33.

Trace and print each set of letters.

A

a

B

b

C

c

Trace each word.

Printing

ALIEN

alien

BARN

barn

COOKIES

cookies

Trace and print each set of letters.

D

d

E

e

F

f

Printing

Trace each word.

DOG

dog

EAGLE

eagle

FLOWER

flower

Trace and print each set of letters.

G

g

H

h

I

i

Trace each word.

GEMS

gems

HOUSE

house

IGUANA

iguana

Trace and print each set of letters.

J

j

K

k

L

l

Trace each word.

JUICE

juice

KITE

kite

LAMP

lamp

Printing

If your child is struggling, try repeating the word out loud first, emphasizing the letter sound. If they still can't guess the letter, point to it from the letter boxes on top and have them copy it.

Print the first letter of each word.

a b c

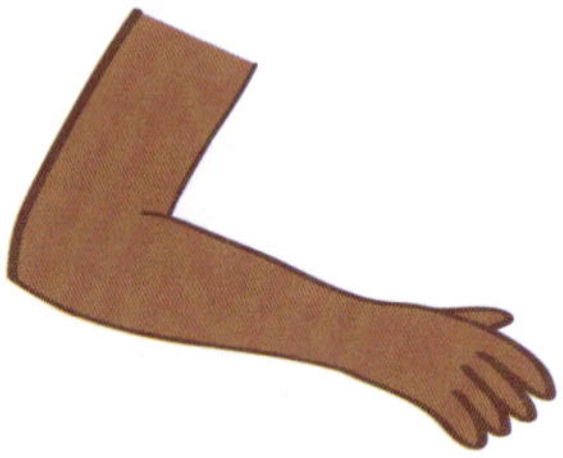

___rm

___vocado

___oot

___ox

___abbage

___an

Print the first letter of each word.

d e f

___og

___onut

___el

___ggplant

___ruits

___lower

Print the first letter of each word.

g h i

__irl

__lobe

__en

__ot dog

__ce

__nsect

Print the first letter of each word.

j k l

_eans

_ug

_angaroo

_oala

_eaves

_obster

Print the first letter of each word.

m **n** **o**

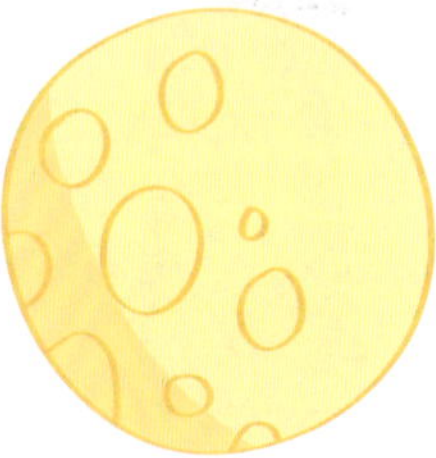

___oon

___onkey

___ut

___est

___ctopus

___wl

Print the first letter of each word.

p q r

__lanet

__izza

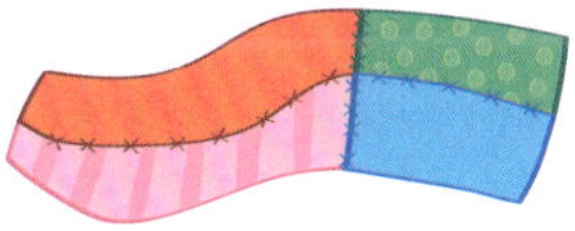

__uilt

__ueen

__ocket

__accoon

Connect each word to the matching picture.

 • • egg

• • globe

 • • insect

 • • apple

 • • worm

 • • clock

Connect each word to the matching picture.

 • • bee

 • • robot

 • • book

 • • arrow

 • • pizza

 • • ice

Connect each word to the matching picture.

 Moon

 hat

 bird

 juice

 flower

 fish

Connect each word to the matching picture.

can

alien

onion

pencil

donut

leaves

Trace and print the number **0**.

Trace and print the word **zero**.

zero

Circle the domino with **zero** dots.

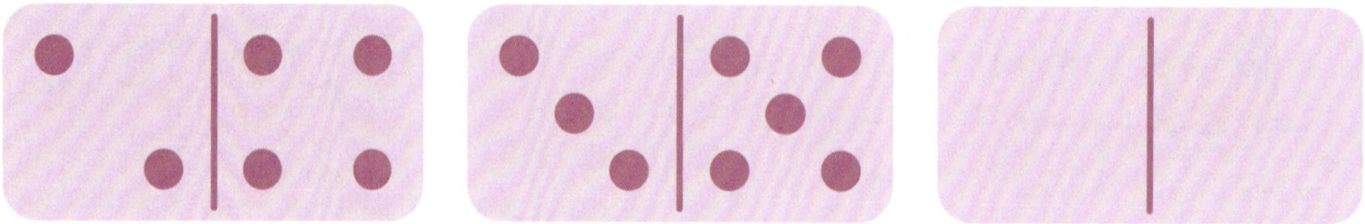

Circle the vase with **0** flowers.

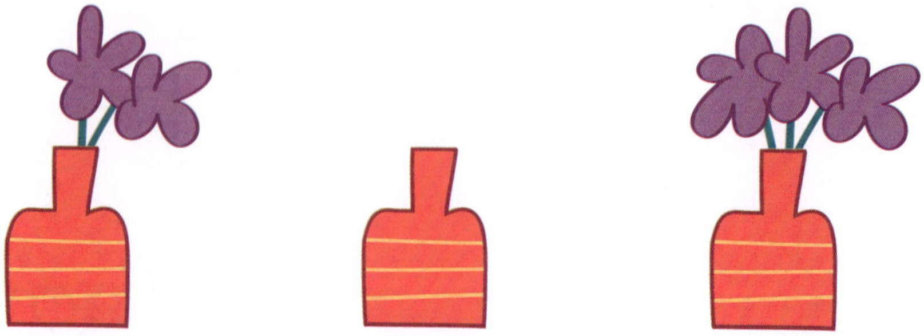

Trace and print the number **1**.

Trace and print the word **one**.

one

Circle the domino with **one** dot.

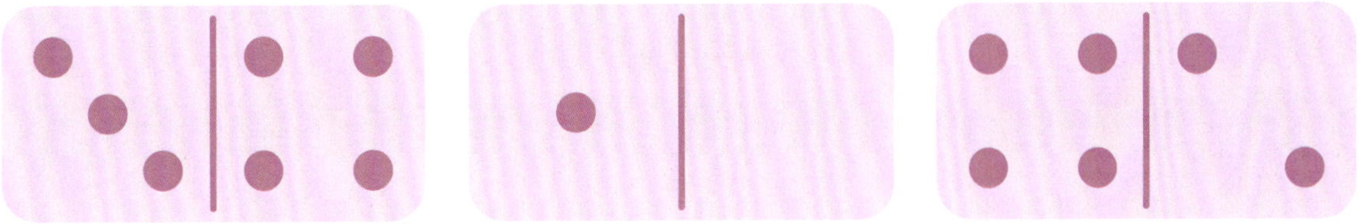

Circle the T-shirt with **1** lightning bolt.

The Number 1

If tracing the numbers with a pen or pencil is too difficult for your child, they can trace the lines with their index finger first.

The Number 2

Trace and print the number **2**.

Trace and print the word **two**.

two

Circle the domino with **two** dots.

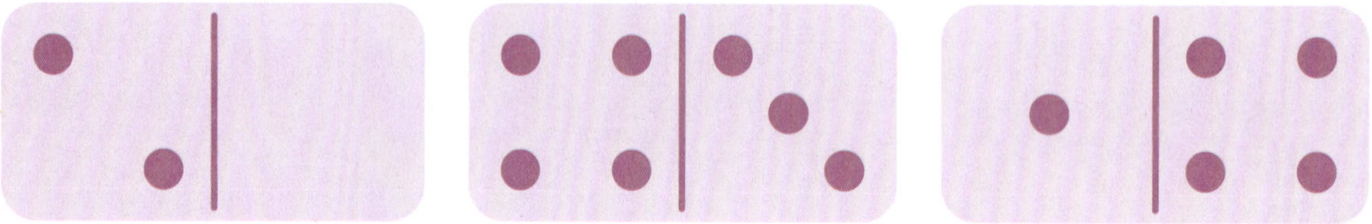

Circle the raccoon with **2** tail stripes.

To make it easier, your child can count the dots on each domino with their fingers. They can also circle each dot one by one and count out loud. To make it harder, they can count the dots in their head.

Trace and print the number **3**.

Trace and print the word **three**.

three

Circle the domino with **three** dots.

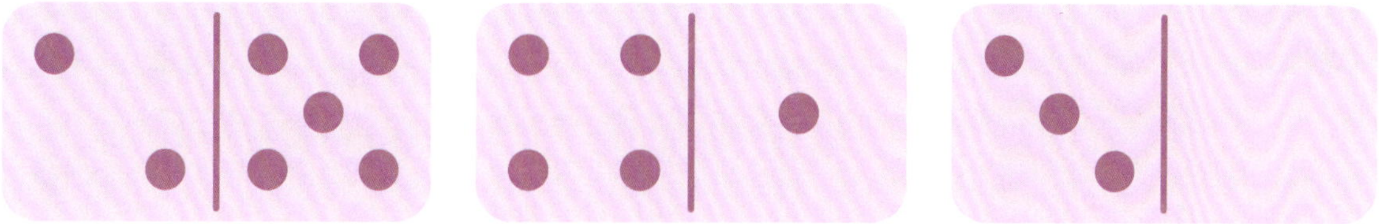

Circle the slice of pizza with **3** pieces of pepperoni.

Trace and print the number **4**.

Trace and print the word **four**.

four

Circle the domino with **four** dots.

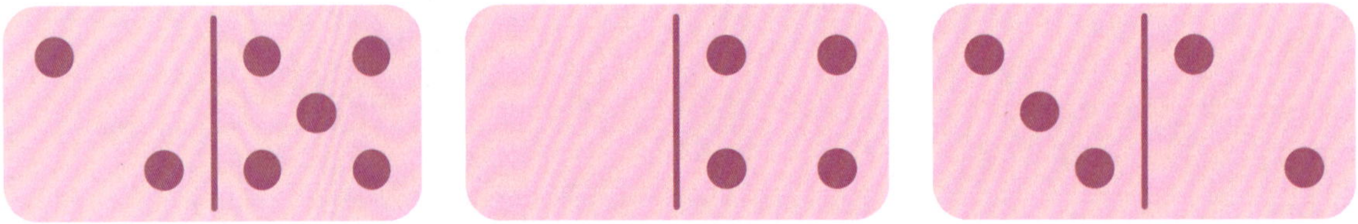

Circle the ladybug with **4** spots.

Trace and print the number **5**.

Trace and print the word **five**.

Circle the domino with **five** dots.

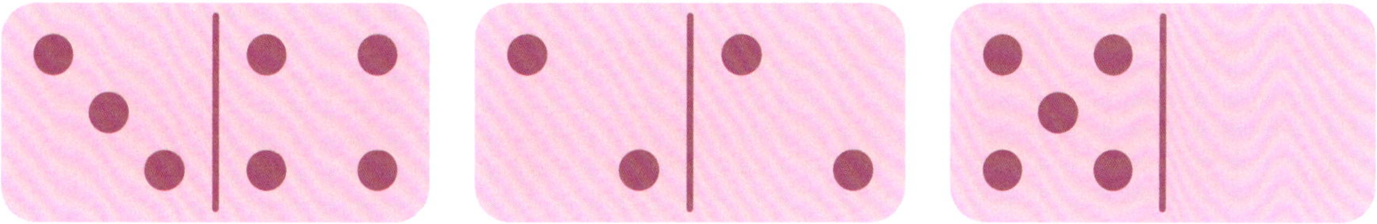

Circle the cup with **5** pencils.

The Number 6

Trace and print the number **6**.

666

Trace and print the word **six**.

six

Circle the domino with **six** dots.

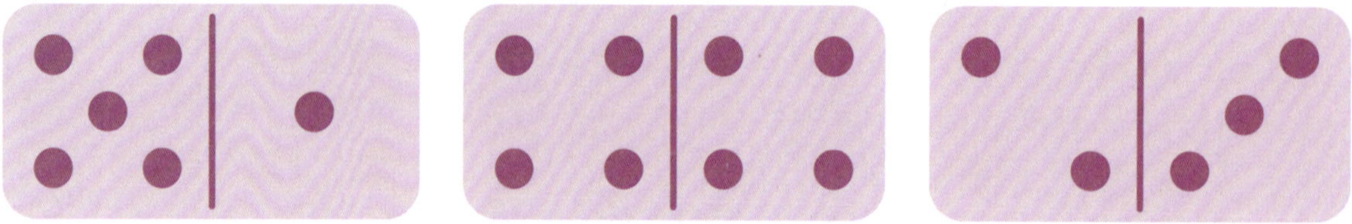

Circle the kettle with **6** dots.

The Number 7

Trace and print the number **7**.

7 7 7

Trace and print the word **seven**.

seven

Circle the domino with **seven** dots.

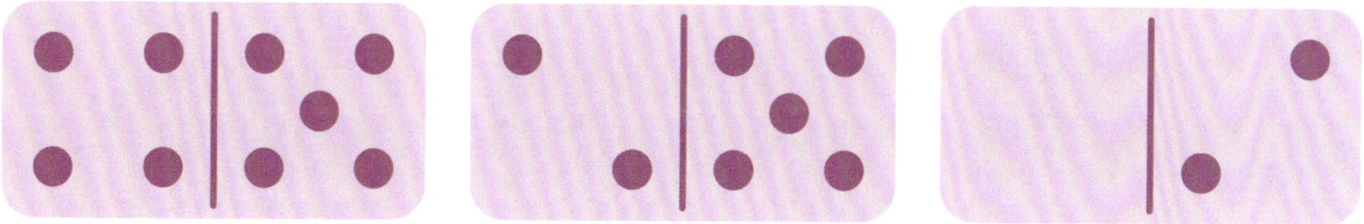

Circle the jellyfish with **7** tentacles.

What is a shark's favourite sandwich?

Peanut butter and jellyfish!

The Number 8

Trace and print the number **8**.

8 8 8

Trace and print the word **eight**.

eight

Circle the domino with **eight** dots.

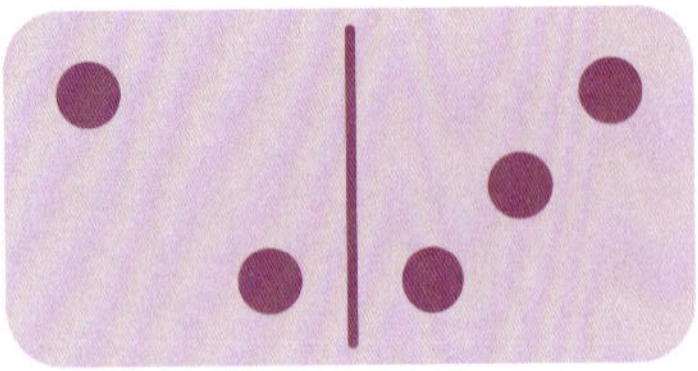 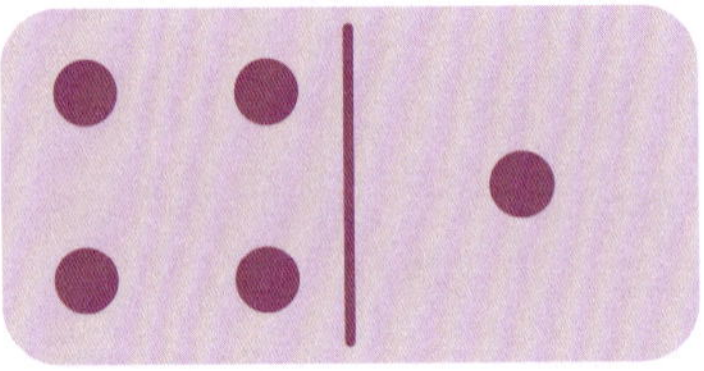 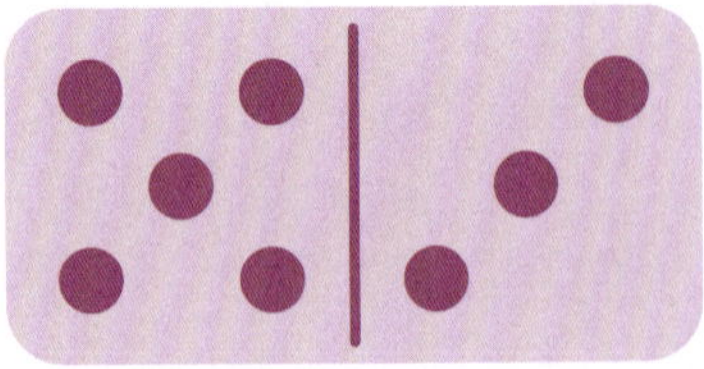

Circle the iguana with **8** spines on its back.

Trace and print the number **9**.

9 9 9

Trace and print the word **nine**.

nine

Circle the domino with **nine** dots.

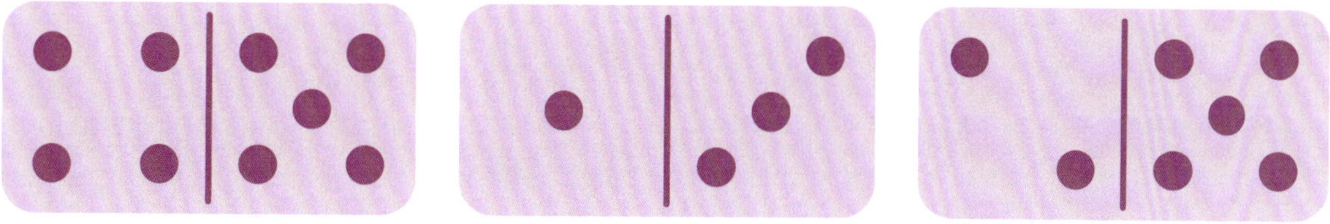

Circle the basket with **9** dots.

The Number 10

Trace and print the number **10**.

10 10

Trace and print the word **ten**.

ten

Circle the domino with **ten** dots.

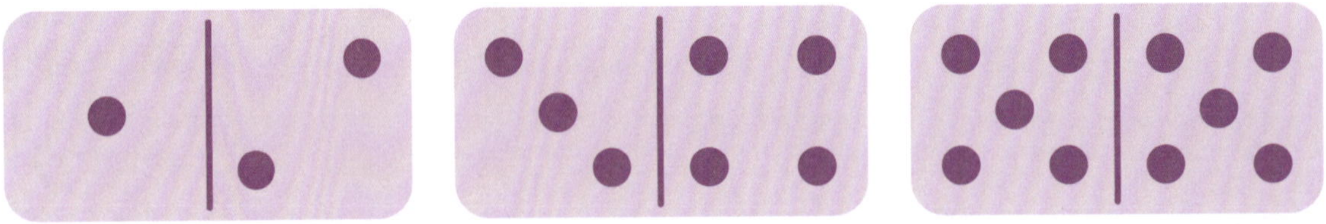

Circle the bush with **10** yellow flowers.

Trace and print the number **11**.

11

Count and colour the apples.

Trace the word **eleven**.

eleven

Trace and print the number **12**.

12

Count and colour the eggplants.

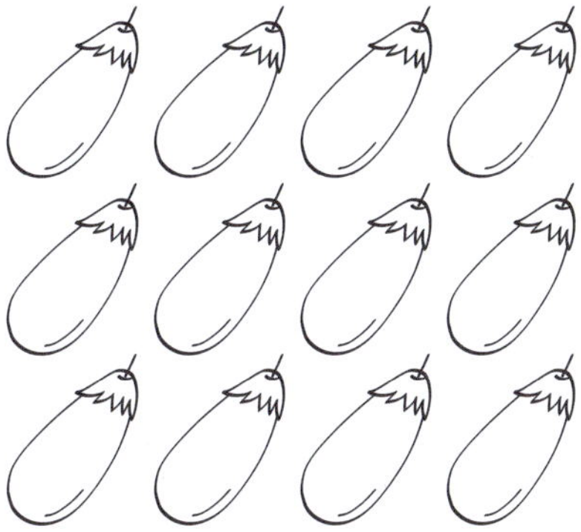

Trace the word **twelve**.

twelve

Trace and print the number **13**.

13

Count and colour the feathers.

Trace the word **thirteen**.

thirteen

Trace and print the number **14**.

14

Count and colour the glasses.

Trace the word **fourteen**.

fourteen

Trace and print the number **15**.

15

Count and colour the wrenches.

Trace the word **fifteen**.

fifteen

Trace and print the number **16**.

16

Count and colour the carrots.

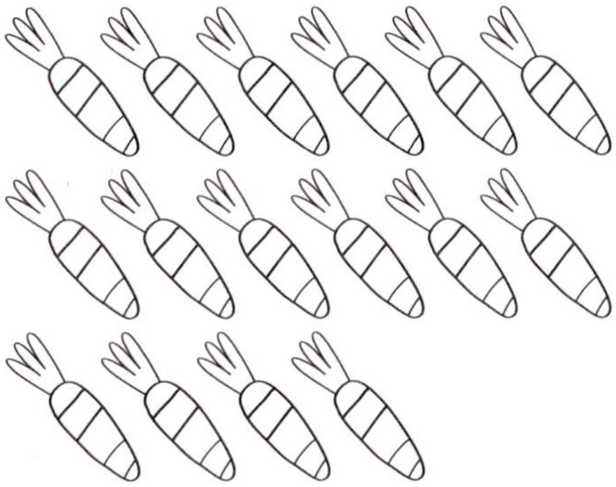

Trace the word **sixteen**.

sixteen

Trace and print the number **17**.

17

Count and colour the flowers.

Trace the word **seventeen**.

seventeen

Trace and print the number **18**.

18

Count and colour the ice cream cones.

Trace the word **eighteen**.

eighteen

Trace and print the number **19**.

19

Count and colour the paintbrushes.

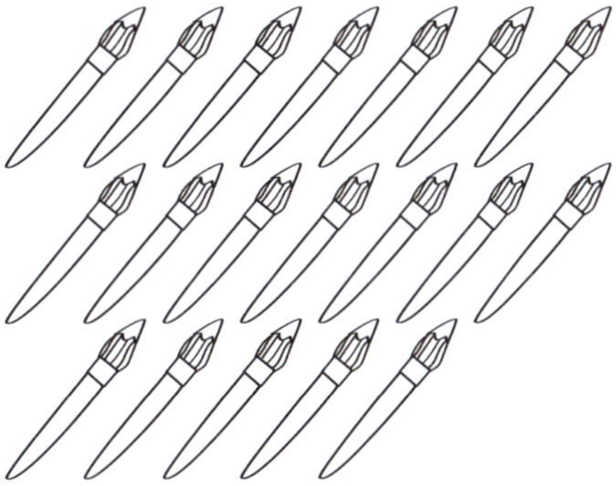

Trace the word **nineteen**.

nineteen

Trace and print the number **20**.

20

Count and colour the pumpkins.

Trace the word **twenty**.

twenty

Count the dots, then trace the numbers 11 to 20.

11	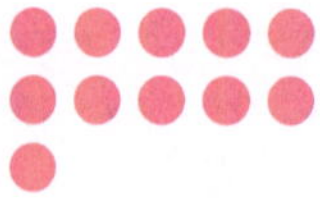	11	11	11	11
12	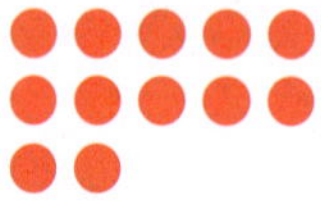	12	12	12	12
13		13	13	13	13
14	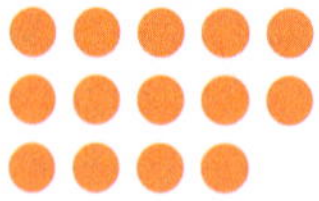	14	14	14	14
15		15	15	15	15
16	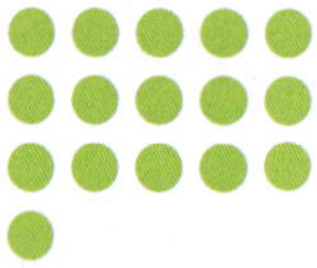	16	16	16	16
17		17	17	17	17
18	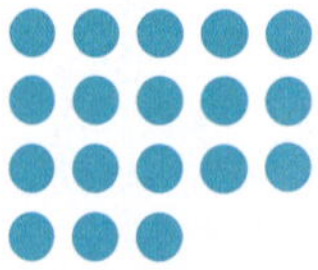	18	18	18	18
19	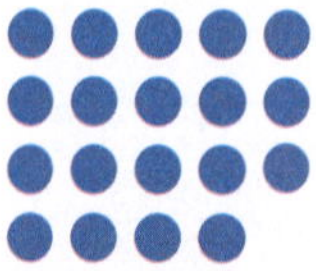	19	19	19	19
20	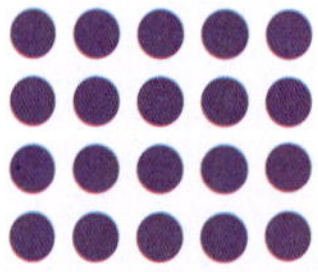	20	20	20	20

Print the numbers 11 to 20.

11
12
13
14
15
16
17
18
19
20

If your child is struggling, they can cross off the objects one by one or say each number out loud as they count the items in each group.

Count each group and draw a line to the matching number.

14

11

13

17

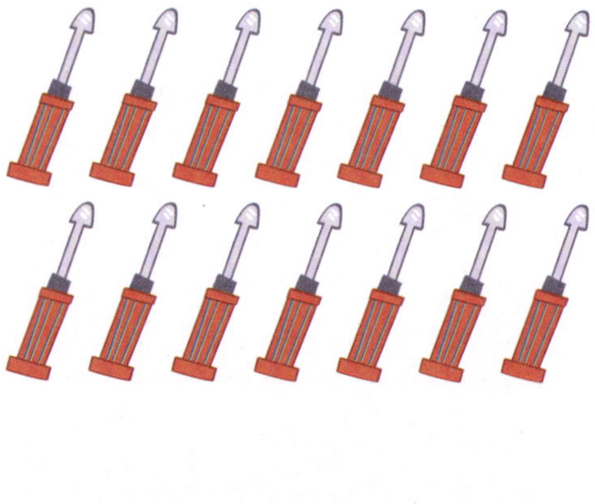

Count each group and draw a line to the matching number.

18

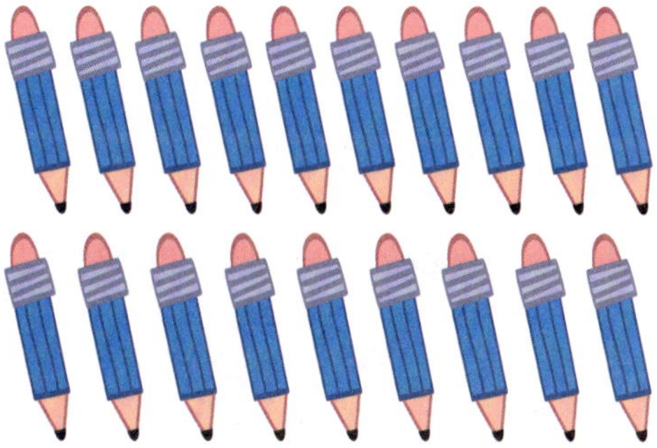

15

19

12

Ask your child which group has the fewest objects and which has the most.

Count each group and write the number in the box. Circle the group that has more items. The first one is done for you.

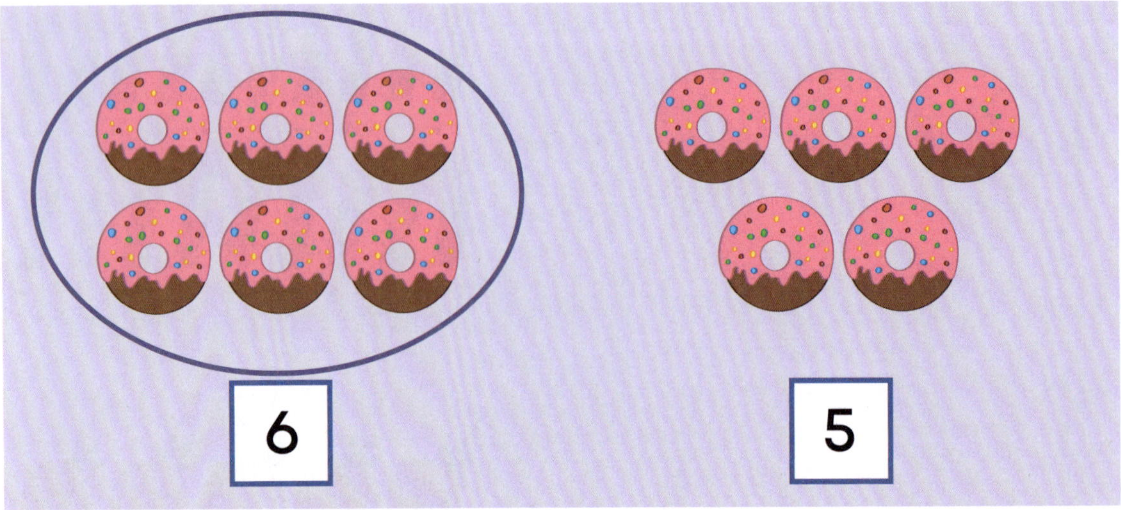

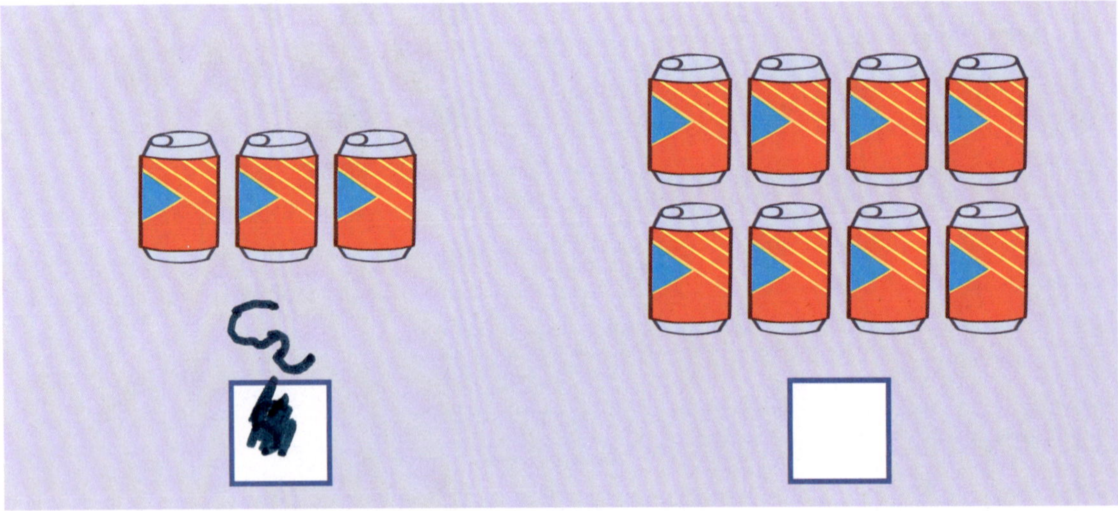

Count each group and write the number in the box. Circle the group that has fewer items. The first one is done for you.

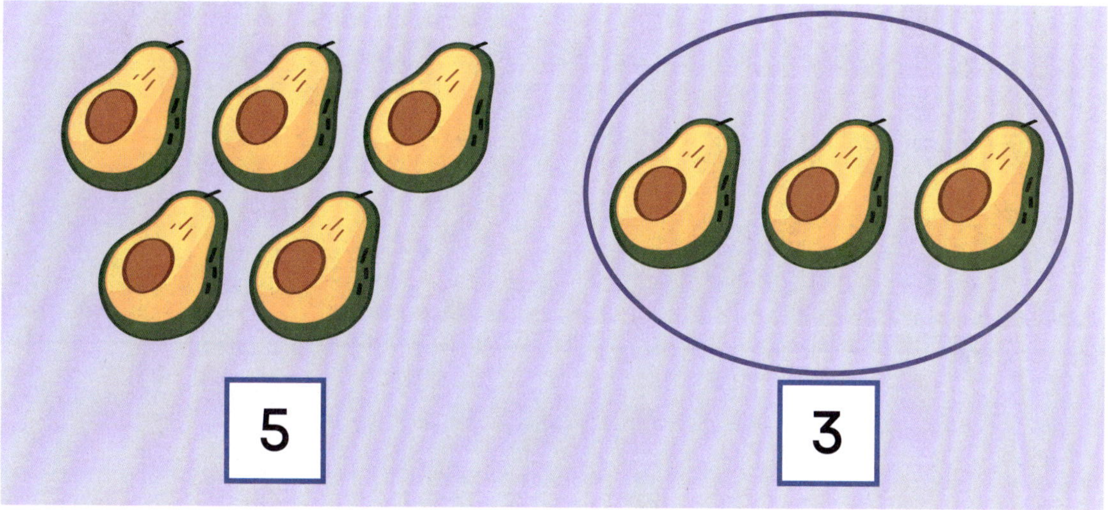

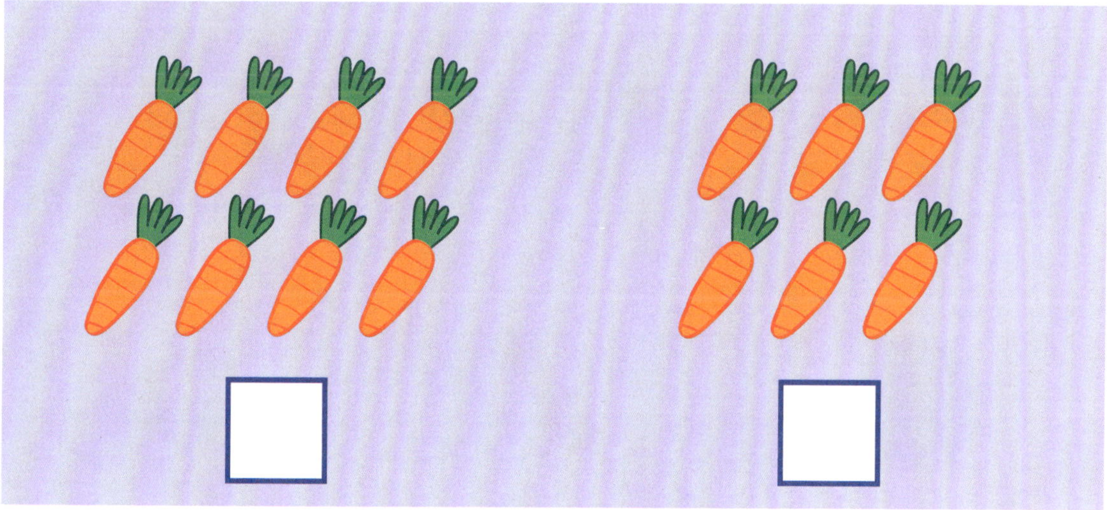

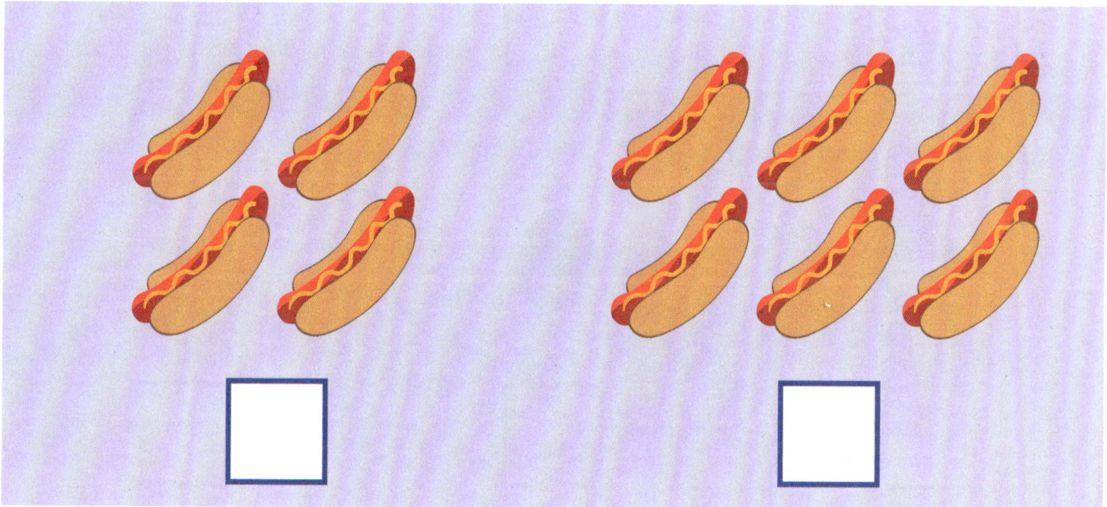

Count each group and write the number in the box.
The first one is done for you.

4

Count each group and write the number in the box.
The first one is done for you.

8

Explain to your child that the easiest way to add is to begin with the larger number and add the smaller number.

Add the numbers.

+

If you have **3 purple** flowers and **2 pink** flowers, how many flowers do you have in total?

3+2 = ____

+

If you have **1 red** apple and **3 green** apples, how many apples do you have in total?

1+3 = ____

+

If you have **1 blue** cup and **1 orange** cup, how many cups do you have in total?

1+1 = ____

+
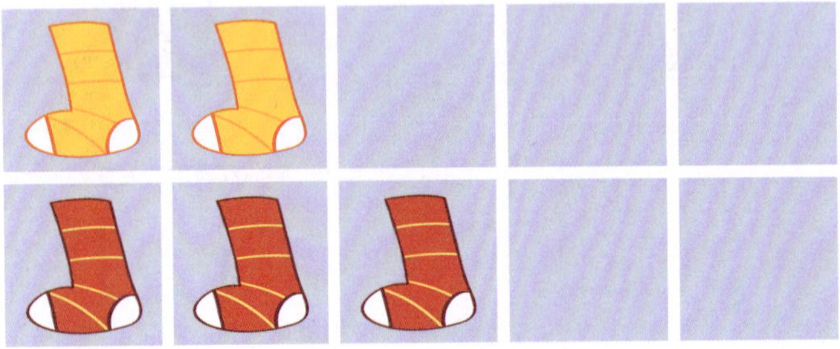

If you have **2 yellow** socks and **3 red** socks, how many socks do you have in total?

2+3 = ____

+

If you have **2 pink** ice cream cones and **1 green** ice cream cone, how many ice cream cones do you have in total?

2+1 = ____

Add the numbers.

\+

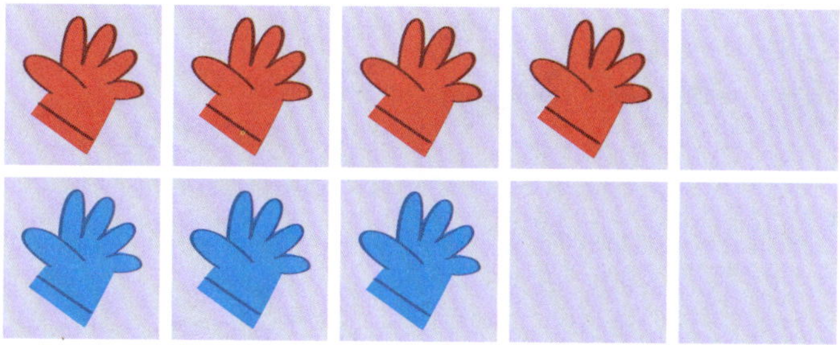

If you have **4 red** gloves and **3 blue** gloves, how many gloves do you have in total?

$4 + 3 =$ ____

\+

If you have **5 green** balls and **5 orange** balls, how many balls do you have in total?

$5 + 5 =$ ____

\+

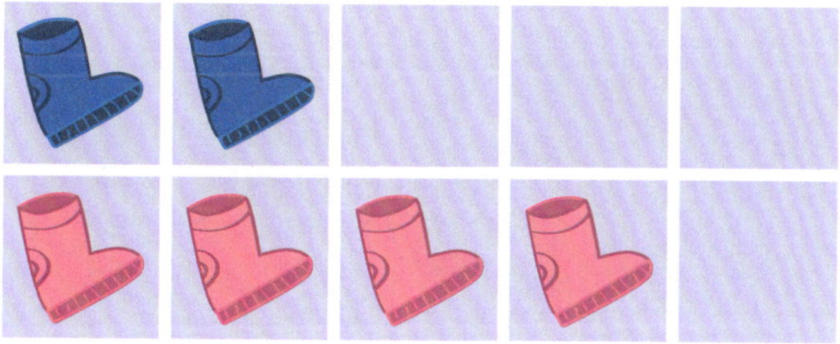

If you have **2 blue** boots and **4 pink** boots, how many boots do you have in total?

$2 + 4 =$ ____

\+

If you have **5 purple** cars and **3 green** cars, how many cars do you have in total?

$5 + 3 =$ ____

\+

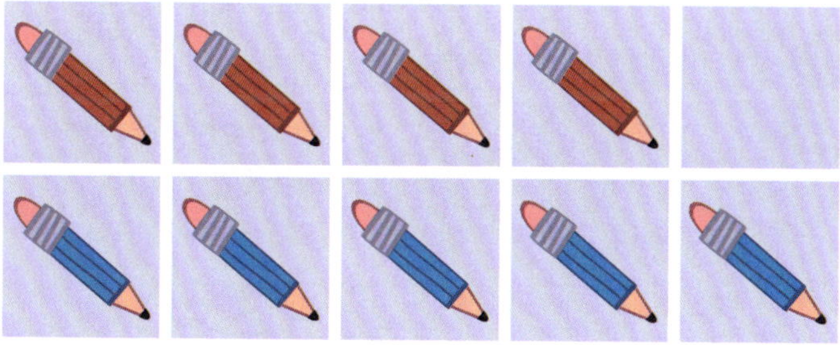

If you have **4 red** pencils and **5 blue** pencils, how many pencils do you have in total?

$4 + 5 =$ ____

Your child can cross off the objects one by one to help them subtract.

Subtract the numbers.

−

Count the birds.
Take away 2.
How many birds are left?

5 − 2 = ____

−

Count the flowers.
Take away 1.
How many flowers are left?

3 − 1 = ____

−

Count the fish.
Take away 2.
How many fish are left?

4 − 2 = ____

−

Count the raspberries.
Take away 3.
How many raspberries are left?

5 − 3 = ____

−

Count the frogs.
Take away 2.
How many frogs are left?

3 − 2 = ____

Subtract the numbers.

−

Count the leaves.
Take away 1.
How many
leaves are left?

$4 - 1 =$ ____

−

Count the ducklings.
Take away 4.
How many
ducklings are left?

$5 - 4 =$ ____

−

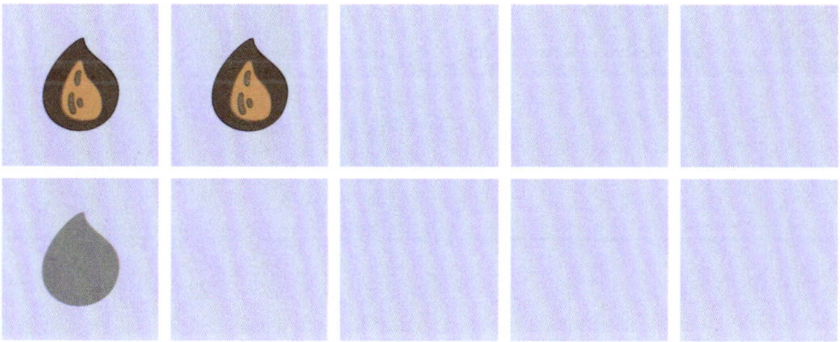

Count the nuts.
Take away 1.
How many
nuts are left?

$2 - 1 =$ ____

−

Count the owls.
Take away 3.
How many
owls are left?

$4 - 3 =$ ____

−

Count the worms.
Take away 1.
How many
worms are left?

$5 - 1 =$ ____

There are different ways to visualize number facts. You can use a number line or a ruler to illustrate subtraction. Begin at the first number, then jump backwards the correct number of spaces.

Colour the objects to complete the patterns. The first one is done for you.

Circle the object that doesn't belong in each pattern. The first one is done for you.

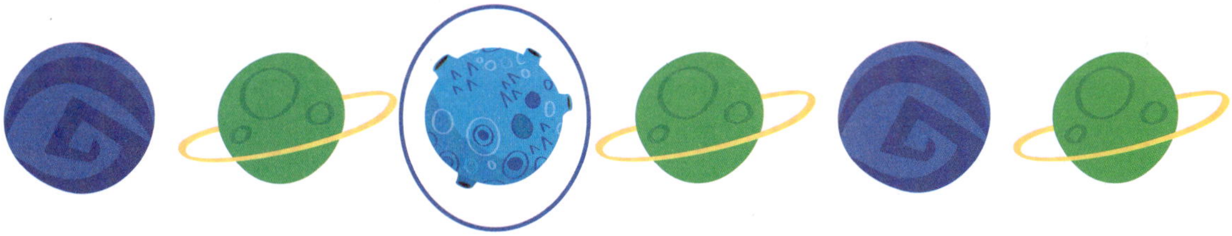

Copy each shape on the grid. Then, count the number of sides and circle the correct number. The first one is done for you.

square

0 1 2 3 4 5

triangle

0 1 2 3 4 5

rectangle

0 1 2 3 4 5

diamond

0 1 2 3 4 5

pentagon

0 1 2 3 4 5

Draw a line from each shape to the matching word.

circle | **square** | **triangle** | **rectangle**

diamond | **heart** | **pentagon** | **star**

What did the circle say to the triangle?

"Without you, my life is pointless!"

Draw a line from each item to the matching colour.

red	**green**	**blue**

green	**red**	**orange**

Draw a line from each item to the matching colour.

purple | pink | yellow

yellow | brown | pink

The number that the big hand points to tells us how many minutes past the hour it is. For example, if the little hand is pointing to 9 and the big hand is pointing to 12, it's 9:00. If the big hand is pointing to 6, it's 9:30.

A clock has two hands: the little hand and the big hand. The little hand tells us the hour and the big hand tells us the minute.

Big: minute hand

Little: hour hand

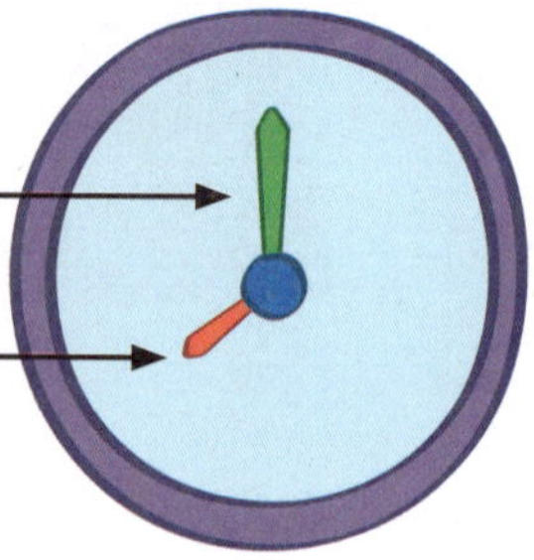

Trace the numbers **1** to **12** on the clock.
Colour the **hour hand red**.
Colour the **minute hand green**.

Look at each clock and fill in the blanks.

The **hour hand** (the little hand) is pointing to _____.

It is _____ o'clock.

The **hour hand** (the little hand) is pointing to _____.

It is _____ o'clock.

The **hour hand** (the little hand) is pointing to _____.

It is _____ o'clock.

The **hour hand** (the little hand) is pointing to _____.

It is _____ o'clock.

Telling Time

The number that the little hand is pointing to tells us what hour it is. For example, if the little hand is pointing to the 3, it is 3:00.

Answers

34

35

44

arm

avocado

boot

box

cabbage

can

45

dog

donut

eel

eggplant

fruits

flower

46

girl

globe

hen

hot dog

ice

insect

47

jeans

jug

kangaroo

koala

leaves

lobster

48

Moon monkey

nut nest

octopus owl

49

planet pizza

quilt queen

rocket raccoon

50

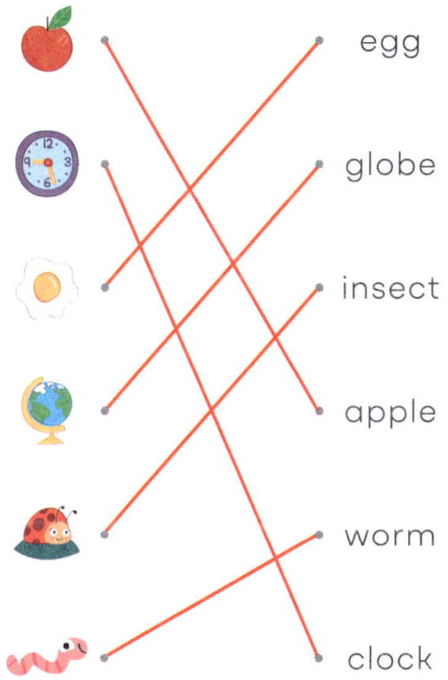

51

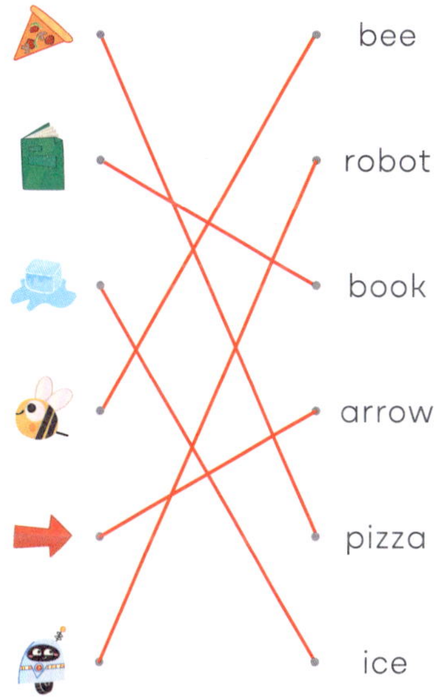

52

53

Answers

54

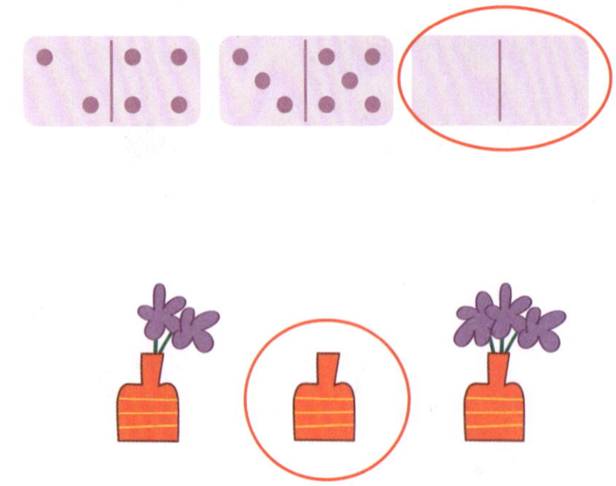

55

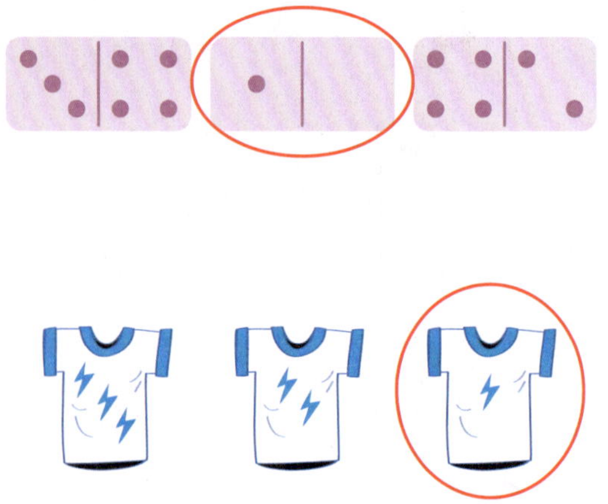

56

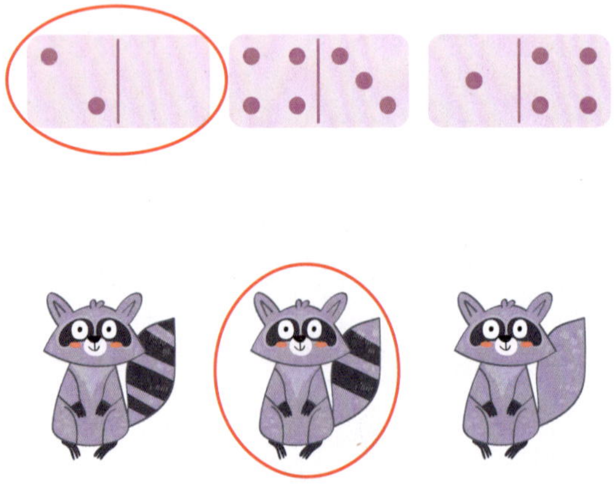

57

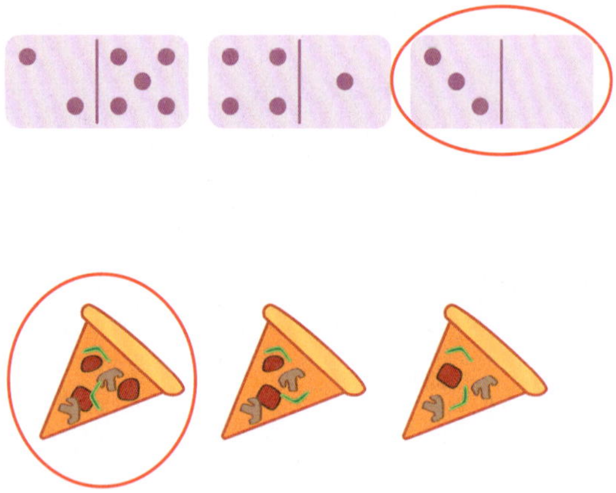

58

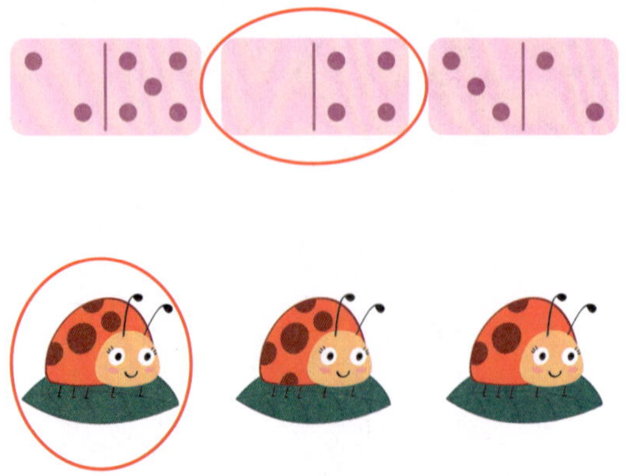

59

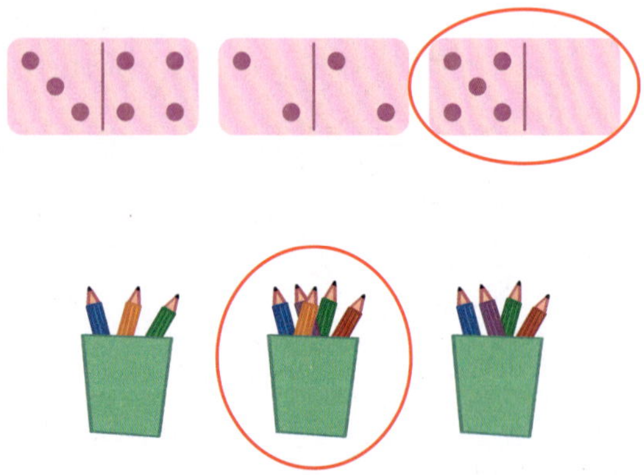

60

61

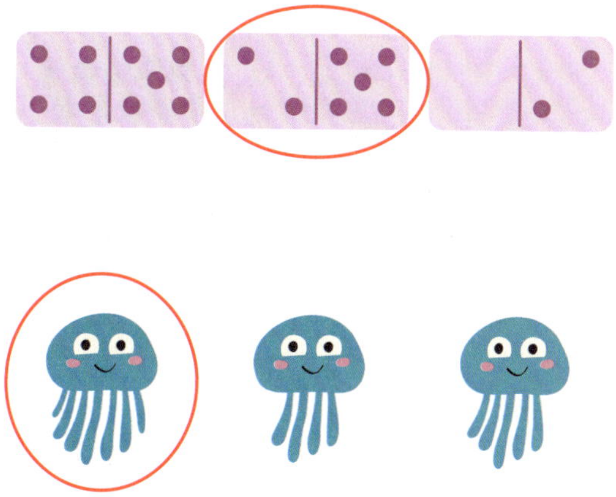

62

63

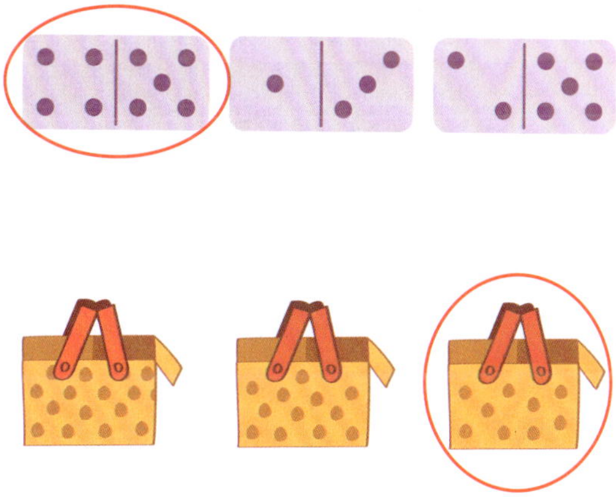

64

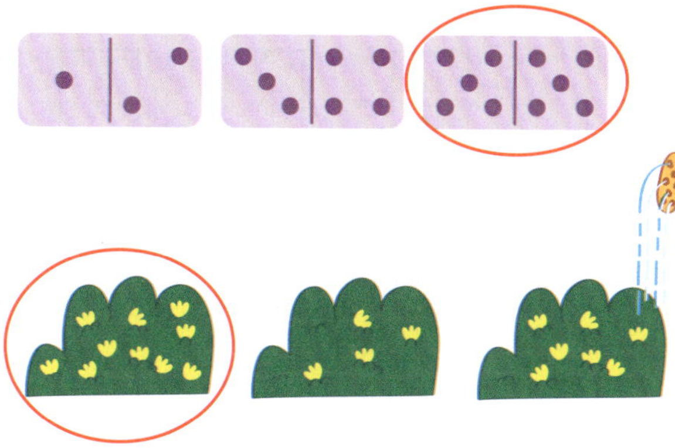

Answers

72

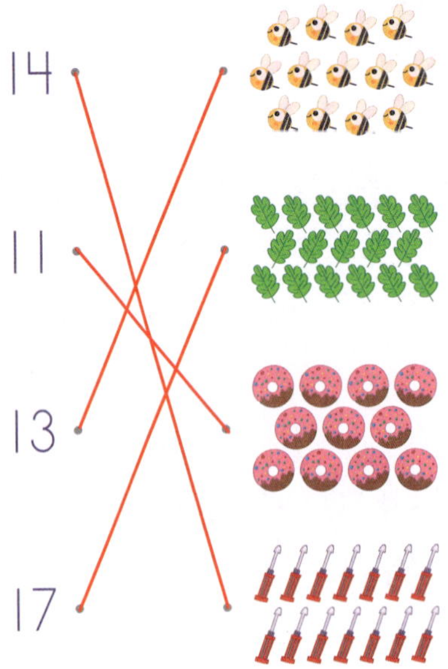

73

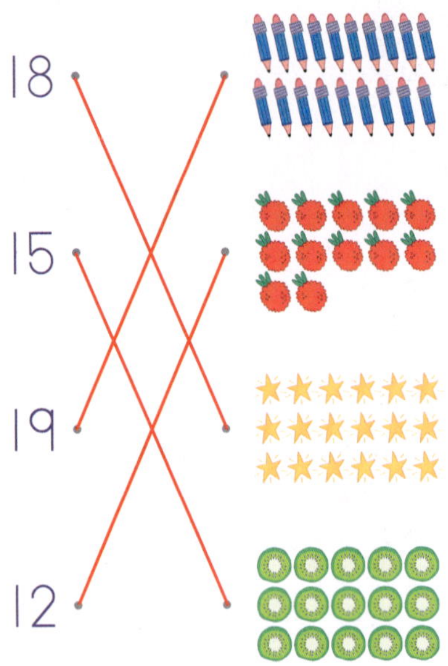

74

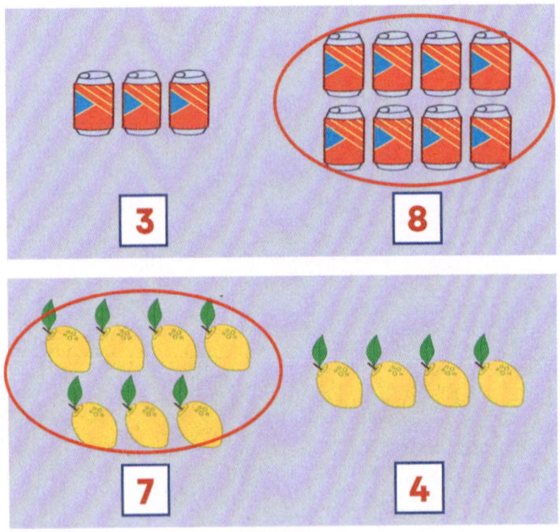

75

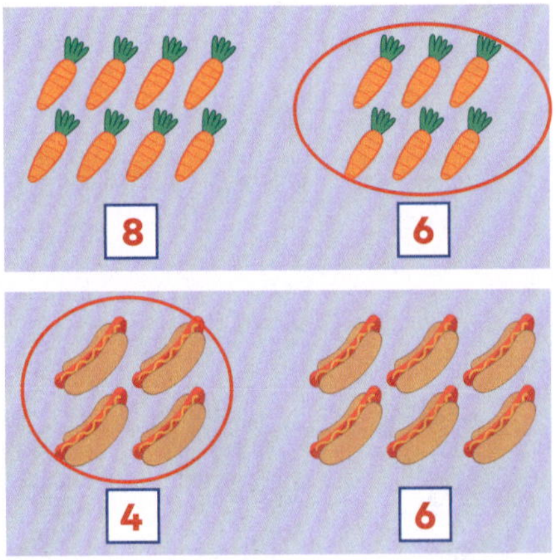

76

77

78

3+2 = 5

1+3 = 4

1+1 = 2

2+3 = 5

2+1 = 3

79

4+3 = 7

5+5 = 10

2+4 = 6

5+3 = 8

4+5 = 9

80

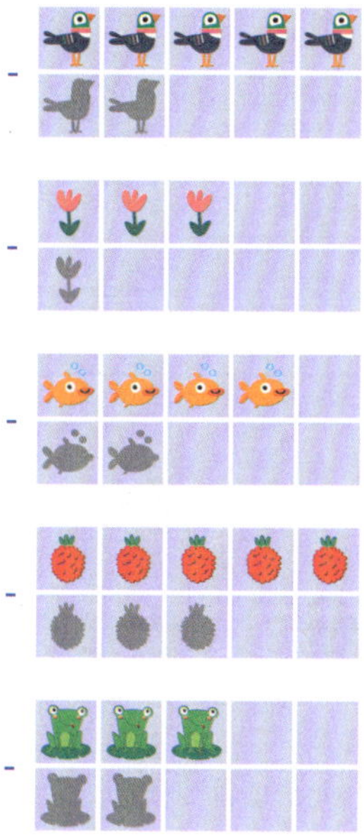

5-2 = 3

3-1 = 2

4-2 = 2

5-3 = 2

3-2 = 1

81

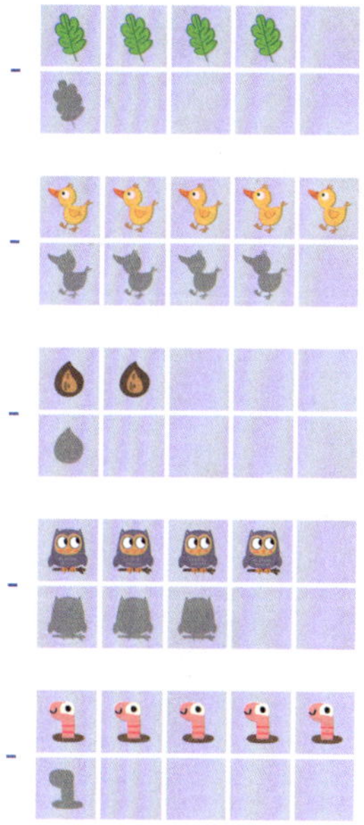

4-1 = 3

5-4 = 1

2-1 = 1

4-3 = 1

5-1 = 4

82

83

Answers

84

triangle

0 1 2 **3** 4 5

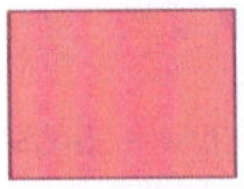
rectangle

0 1 2 3 **4** 5

diamond

0 1 2 3 **4** 5

pentagon

0 1 2 3 4 **5**

85

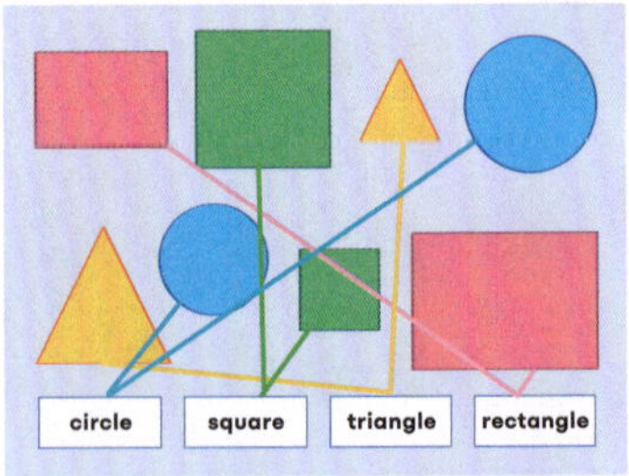

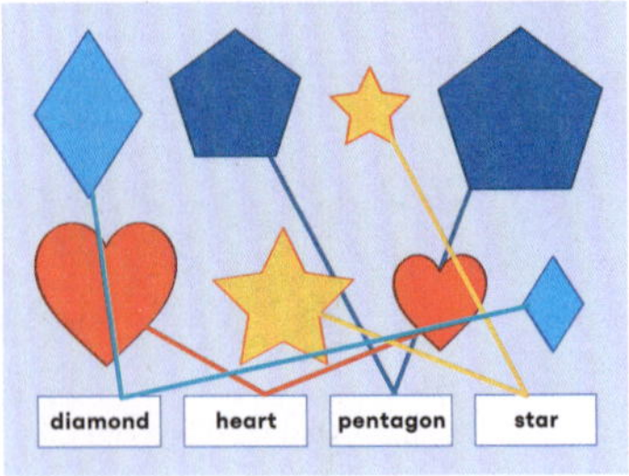

86

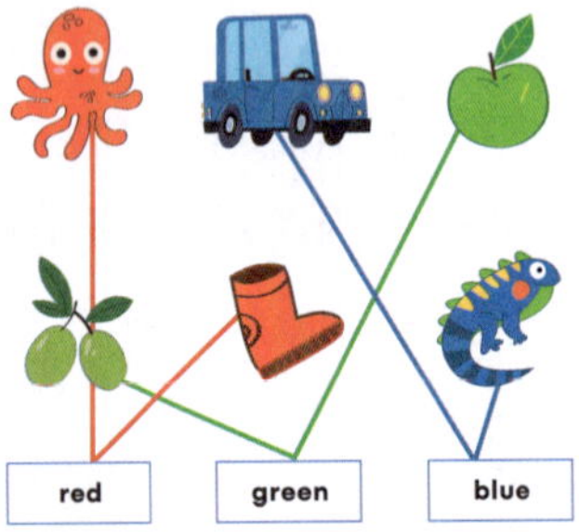

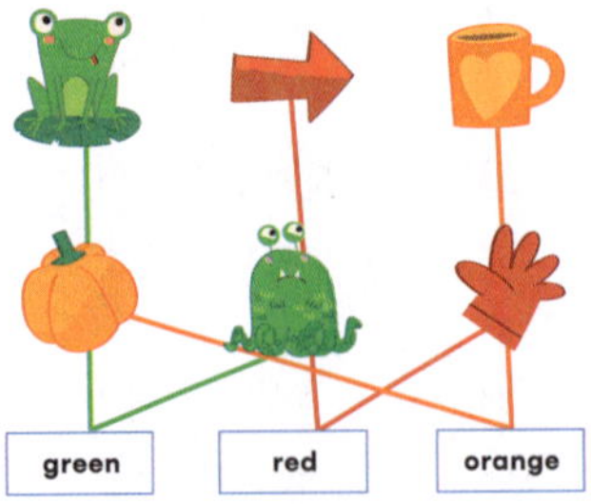

87

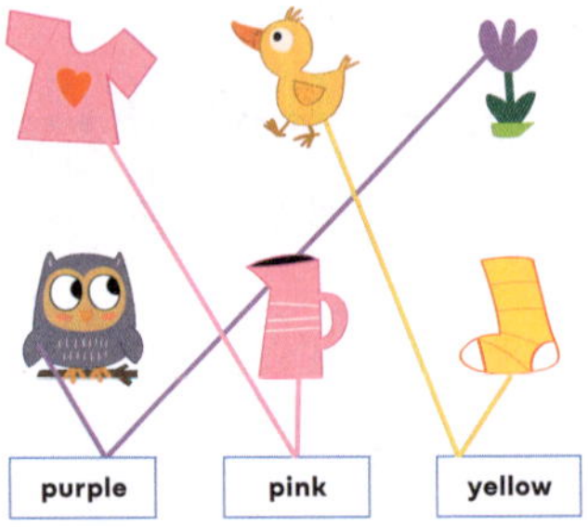

89

The hour hand is pointing to 4.

It is 4 o'clock.

The hour hand is pointing to 1.

It is 1 o'clock.

The hour hand is pointing to 10.

It is 10 o'clock.

The hour hand is pointing to 6.

It is 6 o'clock.